A BRIEF HISTORY OF AMERICA

CONTRADICTIONS & DIVISIONS IN THE UNITED STATES FROM THE REVOLUTIONARY ERA TO THE PRESENT DAY

DOMINIC HAYNES

CONTENTS

Introduction   7

1. Early Divisions in American Politics (1754-1789)   9
2. The Formation of the Two-Party System (1789-1837)   19
3. Manifest Destiny and the Ultimate Regional Fracturing of America (1837-1877)   29
4. The Gilded Age (1870-1900)   37
5. The Empire of the United States (1898-1945)   43
6. The Postwar Era (1945-1980)   55
7. The United States in the Modern Era (1980-Present Day)   61

Other books by Dominic Haynes   67
References   69

© **Copyright - Dominic Haynes 2021 - All rights reserved.**

The content contained within this book may not be reproduced, duplicated or transmitted without direct written permission from the author or the publisher.

Under no circumstances will any blame or legal responsibility be held against the publisher, or author, for any damages, reparation, or monetary loss due to the information contained within this book. Either directly or indirectly. You are responsible for your own choices, actions, and results.

Legal Notice:

This book is copyright protected. This book is only for personal use. You cannot amend, distribute, sell, use, quote or paraphrase any part, or the content within this book, without the consent of the author or publisher.

Disclaimer Notice:

Please note the information contained within this document is for educational and entertainment purposes only. All effort has been executed to present accurate, up to date, and reliable, complete information. No warranties of any kind are declared or implied. Readers acknowledge that the author is not engaging in the rendering of legal, financial, medical or professional advice. The content within this book has been derived from various sources. Please consult a licensed professional before attempting any techniques outlined in this book.

By reading this document, the reader agrees that under no circumstances is the author responsible for any losses, direct or indirect, which are incurred as a result of the use of the information contained within this document, including, but not limited to, — errors, omissions, or inaccuracies.

HOW TO GET A FREE HISTORY EBOOK

Would you like a free copy of a surprise history ebook?

Get free and unlimited access to the below surprise history ebook and all of my future books by joining my Fan Base.

Scan with your camera to join!

INTRODUCTION

There is nothing which I dread so much as a division of the republic into two great parties, each arranged under its leader, and concerting measures in opposition to each other. This, in my humble apprehension, is to be dreaded as the greatest political evil under our Constitution.

— JOHN ADAMS

Contradiction, though an inherently human trait, seems to be a particular theme throughout the history of the United States of America. Within the nation, there have always been two differing visions for how the country should progress, though the shape of these dreams has changed over the years. The same country that loudly and joyously proclaimed that "All men are created equal" in 1776, simultaneously enshrined the fundamentally unequal and cruel institution of slavery in its Constitution a short twelve years later. This nation, touted many times as the "shining city upon the hill" by President Ronald Reagan throughout the 1980s, has been the source of many of modern mankind's luminous achievements, but it has also been the source of many of the modern world's horrors. The history of this country is riddled with the bright stars of human progress and deep stripes of human suffering, a constant tug-of-war between the evils of man and the "better angels" often referenced by President Joe Biden.

These contradictions are found in every crevice of United States history, and the divisions through the populace fracture along socio-economic, regional, ethnic, and religious lines; which are all born out in the wide gulf between the two prevailing political parties of the day. Founding Fathers George Washington and John Adams explicitly warned the young republic about the dangers and divisiveness that two distinct political entities can wreak on a country, and yet even though their warnings came in the salad days of the United States, it was too late. The seeds of the dual-party system were already sown and beginning to bear fruit.

EARLY DIVISIONS IN AMERICAN POLITICS (1754-1789)

Though the history of the indigenous people of the North American continent began centuries before and European colonizers had a sustained presence in the present-day United States for over one hundred years prior, the onset of the French and Indian War in 1754 and the subsequent fallout had much to do with the initial impetus the American colonies felt to break away and construct a separate country. The French and Indian War, which is the name for the North American theater of the more broadly global Seven Years' War, had a deep impact on the formation of the North American continent; British success against the French and their Spanish and Native American allies set Great Britain up as the preeminent empire in the world, and though their final defeat of the French after the Napoleonic wars would drive the final nail into the coffin of the French Empire, the territorial acquisitions gained by the British allowed them to grow and prosper in a way that the conquered French and Spanish Empires were now precluded from. In the terms outlined in the Treaty of Paris of 1763, Great Britain gained control of, alongside other territories around the world, a large swath of land east of the Mississippi River, including Canada, Spanish Florida, and several profitable sugarcane producing islands in the West Indies, previously controlled by Spain and France. French and Spanish influences remained in the North American continent, but it was a feeble whisper compared to the dominating authority ceded to the British.

Despite the rousing military success enjoyed by the British during the Seven Years' War, the empire had taken on a massive financial burden to seize victory. Finding itself deep in war debts, the British government began to search for new streams of revenue, and in a series of laws from 1765 to 1774, they began to levy taxes on the American colonies. These lucrative producers of tobacco, indigo, and other crops, had been largely left alone by the Crown in a policy known as Salutary or Benign Neglect. Regarded as Englishmen by the British government, the colonists had become accustomed to a lack of taxation, since they had no parliamentary representation in London, and saw the new taxes as unjust. An inexorable road of events leading to the Revolution began to unfold; the Stamp Act (1765) which taxed all printed materials was quickly followed by the Townshend Act (1767), taxing all imports of glass, lead, paint, and tea. Enraged colonists attempted to evade the duties placed on them, and a frustrated British government sent troops to enforce the King's Law. Building tensions resulted in the potentially sensationalized Boston Massacre in 1770. There is no doubt that conflict between British regulars and commoners occurred, but who fired first and whether or not it was truly a massacre is unknown. Either way, one of the earliest political divisions in United States History became apparent as the colonies careened towards conflict with the British Empire; one side of colonial society, known as Patriots or "anti-British" were eager for independence while the other side--Loyalists or Tories--were intensely dubious about divorcing from their mother nation, and viewed the Patriots as troublesome firebrands. Though it is tempting to regard the Founding Fathers of the United States as being of one resolute mind, even within the Continental Congress, formed in 1774, the divisions between conservatives like John Jay and John Dickinson and so-called radicals--those who advocated for

American independence--like Thomas Jefferson and John Adams, were rancorous. Jay and Dickinson, fearing the international fallout if the colonies were to leave the British Empire believed reconciliation with Great Britain to be possible. Neither of the men ever signed the Declaration of Independence.

As the rising action of the Revolutionary War sped forward, the British Parliament, in a desperate attempt to bring the colonies to heel and assert their power in the region, passed the Coercive or Intolerable Acts, closing the port of Boston, giving the Crown control over the local government in the colony of Massachusetts, eliminating the right to a trial by one's peers, and forcing the colonists to accommodate British soldiers in their homes (The Quartering Act). Reunification with Britain was increasingly unlikely, and the chasm between the Patriots and the Loyalists opened further, becoming clear that there was no middle ground to be had. In 1775, the first shots were fired at Lexington and Concord, Massachusetts. The Patriots had won the moral high ground on the American Continent. The colonies would not bow to British pressure; it was to be an all-out war, a grim fight for independence.

By 1776, with the Continental Congress in control of governance and independence officially declared, the populace of the colonies continued to remain divided on whether or not independence was beneficial, with their decision largely hinging on how they made their livelihood. The Patriots were mostly yeoman farmers, those who owned the land they cultivated, while Loyalists tended to be those belonging to the merchant or upper class in the cities since they were more likely to have business or even familial ties to the noble classes back in England. However this was not an ironclad rule, and Patriots and Loyalists of many different socio-economic stripes are evident throughout the Revolutionary War Era.

A victory for the ragtag American armies, led by General George Washington, seemed unlikely at best, and the Patriots knew that facing the full might of the British Armed Forces, the preeminent empire in the world, could mean certain death. But unlikely as it may have been, in 1781, the lauded British General Charles Cornwallis, surrendered to the American forces at Yorktown, Virginia. A myth tells the tale of the British troops marching out of Yorktown to the tune of an old English drinking song, "The World Turned Upside Down," but it will never be known for certain if this is a historical fact, despite the utter poetry of the story.

With the war won, the Continental Congress now had to look inward and get to work on the structuring of a nation. A loose constitution, the Articles of Confederation, had been ratified in 1781, but in 1786, its strength was well and truly tested. Disgruntled veterans of the Continental Army had long struggled to get the payment owed them from their time of service, and financial woes among the former soldiers were tragically common. In Massachusetts, a group of these veterans, led by Captain Daniel Shays, rose in violent rebellion after multiple attempts to get debt relief from the Massachusetts government. As more rural farmers in dire financial straits joined the uprising, the governor of Massachusetts assembled the state militia and managed to quash the insurrection, but it became clear that the current government was woefully ill-equipped when it came to financial matters or threats of violence, be they internal or external.

The ensuing Philadelphia Convention of 1787 elected George Washington as the first president of the young nation and began the steady process of drawing up a new constitution. The earliest inklings of political ideology and separate American political philosophies were born during the two years from the initiation of the Philadelphia Convention in 1787 to the ratification of the Constitution in 1789. One group, known as the Federalists and containing the likes of Washington, Adams, and Alexander Hamilton advocated for a stronger central government. Federalist adherents tended to coalesce in the larger cities in New England since the party comprised more of the urban class of merchants and businessmen. On the other side of the aisle was Thomas Jefferson and his Democratic-Republicans, desiring a weaker central government and more state autonomy. These men were mostly farmers from the southern states like Virginia. The differing opinions between these Founding Fathers were instrumental in constructing the delicate balance of power within the United States government. The executive, legislative, and judicial branches were built to enact checks and balances on one another, ensuring that no one faction of the government gains too much power and influence. The Office of the President, the executive branch elected by the people, can approve or veto laws that are created in the legislative branch and retains the power to appoint justices to the judicial branch. In the bicameral United States Congress, where representatives and senators are elected from the states to write laws, they have the power to impeach the president or the justices of the Supreme Court, if their actions are deemed unconstitutional. The final branch, the Supreme Court, or judicial branch is appointed by the executive branch, decides if laws created by the legislative branch are constitutional.

One of the main issues that the Federalists and the Democratic-Republicans clashed on was slavery. Recognizing the inherent contradiction of a nation that declared freedom espousing the tyrannical institution of slavery, a few of the Founding Fathers like Benjamin Franklin and the aforementioned Hamilton, were interested in the gradual abolition of the practice. Southern representatives pushed back, arguing that their farms could not economically thrive without the unpaid labor of enslaved people. Furthermore, when deciding how to calculate taxation and representation within government, the southern representatives, recognizing that northern states had larger populations of eligible voters (i.e., white, property-owning males), pushed to have their slaves counted among the population of southern states. The grim Three-Fifths Compromise was born; allowing southern states to count every five enslaved people as three people. Since the number of representatives allowed per state in the House of Representatives is based on population, this ensured the south would have favorably lopsided representation in the halls of Congress.

The failure of the Founding Fathers to deal with slavery in the early days of the American Republic would have devastating consequences down the line, and they certainly knew the hypocrisy housed within the

Constitution. As Thomas Jefferson, himself a slave owner, presciently noted when referencing slavery, "But as it is, we have a wolf by the ear, and we can neither hold him nor safely let him go. Justice is in one scale and self-preservation in the other."

2

THE FORMATION OF THE TWO-PARTY SYSTEM (1789-1837)

When George Washington gracefully stepped down from power with his farewell address in 1796, he recognized the cracks forming between the Federalists and the Democratic-Republicans. Warning Americans against the idea of a two-party system, he noted that "cunning, ambitious, and unprincipled men" could utilize the system to "subvert the power of the people." Unfortunately, as his successor, John Adams, stepped forward, many Americans had already decided to align themselves with either the Adam's Federalist party or the Democratic-Republicans, most notably represented by Jefferson. Though Adams was indeed a one-term president, much of the negative rhetoric that still circulates about him can be traced back to the election of 1800 which he ultimately lost to Jefferson.

Controversy swirled during the Adams administration, colored mostly by tensions between the United States, England, and France. Several years after the conclusion of the Revolutionary War, under the Federalist Washington administration, Jay's Treaty was signed between the United States and Britain, with the hopes of easing remaining tensions between the two nations. Unfortunately, this greatly irritated Britain's longtime rival, France, who had been instrumental in the establishment of American independence, and hostility was on the rise between the United States and France. When Adams took office, he sent an American diplomat to France intending to ameliorate the American-French relationship. Met by three French diplomats, X, Y, and Z, who demanded a hefty monetary bribe and a massive loan of ten million dollars before they would even speak with him, the American diplomat refused and left. Called the XYZ Affair in the United States, it inflamed the populace against France and calls for war began. In response, Adams signed the highly unpopular Alien and Sedition Acts. These laws restricted entry to the country and also greatly inhibited the freedom of the press, which reflected poorly on Adams. Ultimately, these widely disliked laws, his decision to send peace envoys to France to avoid war, and the partisan rumors that called him a thin-skinned secret monarchist led to his political defeat at Jefferson's hands in the election of 1800.

Jefferson, the author of the Declaration of Independence, was the first Democratic-Republican president, and his conception of the United States as the ideal agrarian nation has shaped political thought in the United States to this day. Part of his success stems from the unity within the Democratic-Republican Party. The opposing Federalists were hopelessly divided against one another with leaders like Hamilton disagreeing vociferously with Adams. Under Jefferson, the landmass of the United States doubled with the Louisiana Purchase in 1803, a massive acquisition of territory from the French.

THE WAR OF 1812 AND THE DISSOLUTION OF THE FEDERALIST PARTY

Despite Jay's Treaty under the Washington Administration, relations between the United States and Britain had not improved. Due to a costly war with Napoleon in France, Britain was frequently seizing American ships at sea and forcing the crews to serve in the British Navy in a system called impressment. Furthermore, with Jefferson's purchase of the Louisiana Territory, more and more American settlers were pushing westward, greatly infringing on the Native American populations who inhabited these lands. Great Britain, fearful of American expansion into their northern territory of Canada, actively supported Native American hostility towards these new arrivals, angering the American government. Many members of Congress, typically Democratic-Republicans from southern slave states, began to agitate for war against the British Empire, while those, mostly Federalists, from the manufacturing centers of New England greatly opposed the conflict, fearing the disastrous economic impact that would certainly accompany the violence.

Nevertheless, the War of 1812 did eventually break out between the United States and Britain, with American forces invading Canada shortly after President James Madison signed the declaration of war. The war was a massive test for the juvenile United States, with Great Britain seizing the nation's capital of Washington, D.C., and torching several government buildings, most notably the Capitol Building and the White House. However, in 1814, An American naval victory at the Battle of Plattsburgh, the withstanding of the siege of Fort McHenry (the details of which were the inspiration behind the American national anthem, Francis Scott Key's "The Star-Spangled Banner"), as well as future president and then General Andrew Jackson's routing of the British offensive at the Battle of New Orleans helped to restore national confidence following the sacking of the capital city. Ended by the Treaty of Ghent in 1815, Britain effectively won the war by successfully defending its colonies in Canada. However, the United States managed to withstand and repulse invasion from a much larger foreign sovereign, indicating that the young nation was coming into its own power.

Federalist hesitancy to support the war efforts led to many seeing the party as less patriotic and supportive than their Democratic-Republican counterparts, and the party slowly dissolved. For a brief period, awash in the success of having staved off a British invasion, American politics was under single-party rule, a time known as "the Era of Good Feelings." Despite Democratic-Republicans having unilateral control of the federal government, regional differences in the nation began to intensify after the external threat of the British was wiped away. The northern half of the country had slowly been phasing out slave labor since the early days of the Jefferson Administration, favoring industrialization and urban development. Conversely, the southern states had increased their reliance on enslaved people to fuel their economy. Cotton had become the primary crop in the south, and Eli Whitney's invention of the cotton gin in the latter part of the eighteenth century had made processing cotton occur at a much faster speed, meaning that more and more enslaved people were necessary to pick more cotton and keep up with the accelerated production capability.

Residents of northern states were becoming increasingly critical of slavery, and political mobilization was underway to limit the spread of slavery in the western territories. In 1818, Missouri petitioned to become a state and intended to allow slavery within its borders. This sparked heated debates between pro and anti-slavery factions within Congress. It was eventually settled through the Missouri Compromise of 1820: Missouri would be admitted as a slave state alongside the admission of Maine as a free state. Furthermore, Missouri would be the only slave state allowed to exist above the 36º 30' parallel, or Missouri's southern borderline. This compromise was a mere bandaid for the contentious issue of slavery between the northern and southern states would continue to intensify and worsen. Jefferson's wolf was stalking the United States, and the nation would receive its reckoning in due time.

JACKSONIAN DEMOCRACY AND THE FALL OF THE "AMERICAN ARISTOCRACY"

The first six presidents of the United States had all come from highly regarded families, and all of them, except for the last, John Quincy Adams, had been Founding Fathers. It should be noted though that John Quincy Adams was the son of Founding Father and second president, John Adams. There had been a certain genteel quality to the way these men conducted themselves in political campaigns, eschewing openly campaigning for themselves. However, the tense election of 1824 introduced a new element into American political life. In a four-way race between John Quincy Adams, Andrew Jackson, Henry Clay, and William Crawford, no candidate won the majority of the votes necessary to win as laid out in the Twelfth Amendment. Even though Jackson had technically won the most popular and electoral votes, the election was deferred to the House of Representatives and the victory was awarded to John Quincy Adams. Clay, at the time, was the Speaker of the House and when he subsequently garnered a position in Adams' cabinet as the Secretary of State, Jackson furiously decried the whole business as a "corrupt bargain."

Throughout Adams' presidency, Jackson railed against the duplicity of the so-called elites, billing himself as a common man who had been dealt a raw deal by the Washington political establishment. He criticized Adams on every front possible, insisting that his "Tariff of Abominations" greatly benefited the northern states at the expense of the southern states. He stoked indignation against Adams' supposedly lax handling of the Native American Nations, believing that American westward expansion was greatly hampered by their presence. At this time, the makeup of American voters was slowly changing away from white, male property owners, allowing all white males to vote, and Jackson successfully marketed himself to the dissatisfied white males who felt impaired by the Adams presidency.

In 1828, a vicious election season ensued. Jackson had formed his own party, the Democrats, the very same party as today's Democratic party. Meanwhile, the Democratic-Republican Party had largely faded away in the vile political culture leading up to the election, and John Quincy Adams, now billing himself as a member of the new Whig party, went up against Jackson for a second time. This election was not far removed from modern American elections, with endless mudslinging, ad hominem attacks, and constant appeals to the "common man." Finally, at the end of 1828, Andrew Jackson rode a wave of popular discontent into the office, becoming the seventh president.

Much of Jacksonian Democracy looks similar to what is seen in the present-day United States. The hateful campaign between Adams and Jackson cemented the two-party system as a fixture of American politics, while Jackson's espousing of "common man" politics echoes what many American voters look for in their leaders today. In fact, the first nomination convention in American history was held in 1832 for Jackson's reelection campaign. Criticized throughout his terms in office as "King Andrew," and accused of abusing his presidential powers, Jackson transformed the office of the presidency. He utilized the veto more indiscriminately than his predecessors, most notably to veto the Bank Bill in 1832, and greatly increased the power of the executive branch. Jackson's development and implementation of the "spoils system" also set the precedent for modern-day political appointments. Derived from the phrase, "to the victor go the spoils," the spoils system allowed the new president to essentially clean out the government and replace current employees with new ones, loyal to him and his party. This rewarded people with jobs for participating in the party and led to increased party loyalty. Americans now looked for virtue within their political party, rather than within individual men.

In the end, Jackson's ill-fated decision to veto the Bank Bill in 1832 led to the charter of the Second Bank of the

United States lapsing. This coupled with Jackson's economic policies caused financial pain and ruin throughout the nation with the Panic of 1837, a depression that lasted until halfway through the 1840s. Jackson managed to escape political destruction, leaving office in 1837, but his successor and fellow Democrat, Martin Van Buren was not so lucky. Widely lambasted as "Martin Van Ruin," he only served one term and paved the way for the Whigs to take control in the election of 1840.

3

MANIFEST DESTINY AND THE ULTIMATE REGIONAL FRACTURING OF AMERICA (1837-1877)

By 1846, President James K. Polk had annexed Oregon Territory from the British, and in 1848, due to the American defeat of Mexico in the Mexican-American War, the United States took control of California, New Mexico, Arizona, Texas, and a portion of Colorado. That same year, gold was discovered in Sutter Creek, California, and the pace of American expansion westward became decidedly more frenzied. As white settlers moved west, displacing the Native Americans along the way, an idea congealed in the popular narrative: Manifest Destiny. Subscribers to this ideology believed that the United States had been mandated by God to spread capitalism, democracy, and American values and civilization across the entirety of the North American continent.

With the addition of new territories, the potential for new slave or free states threatened to upend the delicate balance of the Union, and political parties began realigning along purely regional lines. The Wilmot Proviso was set forth by Pennsylvania Congressman David Wilmot in hopes to ban slavery from all the territories acquired from Mexico. Unfortunately at the time, the Senate was largely controlled by southern Democrats who struck the bill down. As the Whig party was fading out of significance and Democrats were consolidating in the south, two new and short-lived parties cropped up. While most of the country seemed to be wrapped up with the issue of slavery, the xenophobic and nativist "Know-Nothing" or Native American Party strongly opposed immigration and religious differences in the country. Their rhetoric reflects a lot of what anti-immigration activists will say today, but since the chief immigrant groups at the time were Irish, Italians, and Germans, their ire was largely directed towards those ethnic groups. Since many immigrants, especially from Ireland and Italy tended to be Catholic, Know-Nothing gangs often targeted Catholics, burning churches and spreading anti-Catholic propaganda. In contrast, the Free Soil Party, rising up at roughly the same time, began loudly opposing the expansion of slavery to new states.

In an attempt to diffuse the strain between the north and the south, Henry Clay, the mastermind behind the Missouri Compromise thirty years prior, dreamed up the Compromise of 1850. This admitted California as a free state, allowed slavery in Washington, D.C., but outlawed the slave trade, allowed Utah and New Mexico to decide for themselves if they would be slave or free states, and enacted the controversial Fugitive Slave Act. This made it the legal obligation of every American citizen to report and apprehend escaped enslaved people and denied them the right to a trial by jury. The Fugitive Slave Act was a massive misstep since it now forced those residing in free states to participate in the enforcement of slavery. Citizens could no longer turn a blind eye. Eventually, in political response, former Whigs coupled with Free Soilers in the north formed a new political coalition in 1854, the Republican Party.

With the repealing of the Missouri Compromise in the Kansas-Nebraska Act of 1854, two new states, Kansas and Nebraska, were now allowed to decide for themselves if they were to be free or slave states, rather than having them admitted as free states as they would have been under the Missouri Compromise. Supporters of both sides poured into the states, initiating violent conflicts that dubbed the area "Bleeding Kansas." It was not any more civil in the halls of Congress, where a pro-slavery Democrat from South Carolina, Preston Brooks, beat Republican and abolitionist Charles Sumner with a cane for his anti-slavery remarks.

The differences between the south and the north had become so strident that violence was swiftly becoming the only answer. Aligned under different political parties (Republicans in the north and Democrats in the south), operating other differing economies (an industrial north versus agricultural south), and existing in different societal structures (a burgeoning middle class in the north contrasted with the almost feudal landed gentry in the south), the states were primed for devastating conflict.

THE CIVIL WAR

The election of 1860 pitted Republican Abraham Lincoln against the southern Democrat John C. Breckinridge, with several states that bordered both free and slave states setting up their own unsuccessful Constitutional Party in an attempt to thwart a Republican victory through third-party intervention. Lincoln was victorious, and several southern states, believing that his election spelled the end of slavery for the entire country, seceded in quick succession. The first seven to leave the Union were South Carolina, Florida, Georgia, Alabama, Mississippi, and Louisiana. Forming the

Confederate States of America, and electing Jefferson Davis as the president, they were later joined by Tennessee, Texas, Arkansas, Virginia, and North Carolina.

Lincoln had been comfortable with allowing slavery to languish in the southern states; he had never intended to abolish it completely, the schism between the north and the south that had been building since the earliest days of the nation's founding was finally complete. Through the next five years, the Confederate States and the United States waged a fearful and bloody war on one another, reshaping the landscape of the south and completely altering the nation. During the time of the Civil War, the power of the federal government greatly expanded with legislation like the Habeas Corpus Suspension Act giving the government the power to indefinitely imprison and silence those deemed to be a threat. Slavery was abolished through the Emancipation Proclamation of 1863, though it would take until June 19 of 1865 for the last enslaved people to finally be freed in Galveston, Texas. The country emerged from the conflict, scarred and bruised, but with a new sense of national identity. Though before the Civil War it was common to see the name of the nation written as "These United States," moving forward it is only referred to as "The United States." No longer seen by some as a loose agreement between separate territories, the states were solidly fused as one indivisible nation.

RECONSTRUCTION

After Lincoln's untimely assassination in April of 1865 and Confederate General Lee's submission to Union General Ulysses S. Grant at Virginia's Appomattox Courthouse in June of the same year, the long road to recovery began. Andrew Johnson, a southerner, was now president, and the United States government was walking a fine line between redressing the wrongs of slavery and bringing the former Confederate States back into the fold. Yet, the south was not so keen to yield. Resenting their northern "occupiers" sent down by the federal government, a series of laws in multiple southern states from 1865 to 1866 known as the "Black Codes" sought to control formerly enslaved people through the legal system. However, anger in the northern states over these restrictive laws led to the Reconstruction Act in 1867, which outlined the terms for which states were to be readmitted to the Union, including military rule until new governments could be established. Formerly enslaved men were enfranchised, which terrified the white population. Black men were elected to state, local, and federal government positions, laws against racial discrimination were passed, and the first state-funded school systems in the south were established. Many formerly Democrat states became Republican states as a new bloc of voters had their say.

Straining against Union occupation and bitter over the perceived power lost during Reconstruction, southern white Democrats were increasingly turning to violence to maintain control through organizations like the Ku Klux Klan (KKK). Eventually, in an attempt to ease the bloodshed and tensions in the south, Republican presidential candidate Rutherford B. Hayes reached a compromise with Democrats in Congress. They agreed to certify his election if he agreed to end Reconstruction in the South.

With Hayes formally ending Reconstruction in 1877, the backlash against Black citizens in the south was severe, and eventually, all of the ground gained for Black liberation during Reconstruction would be rapidly rolled back when Union troops withdrew. Though the Civil War had ended with a victory for the Union, the divisions between the regions had not eased or erased.

4

THE GILDED AGE (1870-1900)

After the horrors of the Civil War, the effects of the Second Industrial Revolution on the United States economy became apparent, leading to an impressive period of expansion. Much like the First Industrial Revolution that was unfolding during the nation's founding, the Second Industrial Revolution brought forth technologies that would change the way Americans worked, lived, and operated in the world. Notable advancements of the time include the telephone, refrigeration, and the Bessemer process for manufacturing steel. The Bessemer process allows the steel to be mass-produced, greatly lowering the cost and the speed at which the product can be created. More plentiful, less expensive steel led to an explosion in the railroad industry, and vast networks of rail lines were thrown down from the Atlantic to the Pacific. The new, metallic network linking the country closed geographic distances and also led to the standardization of time across the nation, to avoid train collisions and allow for more efficient scheduling. The country seemed to be on the move as cities exploded with the increased opportunity for jobs and tall, multi-storied buildings with steel frames--America's first skyscrapers--began to dot the horizons of larger cities like Chicago and New York.

All of this progress would seem like the United States was headed into a Golden Age, but American writer, Mark Twain, saw the truth. In his 1873 novel *The Gilded Age: A Tale of Today*, he utilized satire to criticize the horrifying wealth inequality that was plaguing the land. Rather than a Golden Age, the United States was experiencing a Gilded Age: glittering in its appearance, but concealing the rotten truth below. As the nation's wealth grew, it was only falling into the hands of the top one percent of the country. A small upper class--the likes of Andrew Carnegie, Cornelius Vanderbilt, and John D. Rockefeller--had swelling bank accounts and palatial homes while the much larger lower classes lived in cramped, dirty, and poorly lit tenement houses and operated under dangerous and difficult working conditions.

There were no labor laws or worker protections to speak of at the time, and workers frequently fell victim to unlivable wages, unhygienic work sites, and life-altering accidents. In response to this, the first labor movements and union mobilization began. Employers, resisting new union demands for better pay and safer working conditions would often respond negatively to strikes, which would sometimes turn violent and deadly, like the Homestead Strike in 1892 at a Carnegie steel plant in Pennsylvania. When the plant's manager, Henry Frick, used Pinkerton Detectives--a private police force at the time--to break the strike, it turned into a bloody twelve-hour shootout between the Pinkertons and the steelworkers. This was particularly shocking to the public since the owner of the plant, Andrew Carnegie, was often seen as a champion of labor and saw it as his duty as a wealthy man to assist those who had less; he elucidated this in his book *The Gospel of Wealth.*

Carnegie's mindset placed him squarely in the minority. A prevailing school of thought at the time was Social Darwinism, a sociological application of Darwin's theory of "survival of the fittest." Many believed that those on the top of society, the wealthy and privileged, were there because they were genetically superior to the poorer inhabitants of the tenement houses. This way of thinking wound its way insidiously through the American psyche at this time. It was used to uphold the racist idea that white people of Western European descent were more highly evolved than Black Americans, Asian Americans, Native Americans, or white people of Eastern European descent. Social Darwinism upheld sexist and misogynist ideas of women being the weaker sex and ultimately led to the rise of eugenics in the United States. These ideas were reflected in the laws; the Chinese Exclusion Act in 1882 barred Chinese immigrants from entering the country, the Dawes Act of 1887 took land from Native Americans, and Plessy vs. Ferguson in 1896 set judicial precedent for segregation, ruling that "separate but equal" was constitutional. Social Darwinism gave rise to racist, sexist, misogynist, nativist, xenophobic, and imperialistic ideas that the country still grapples with today.

Politically, at this time, the United States government was highly corrupt, slow, and ineffective. A slew of forgettable presidents passed in and out of office--none of whom managed to capture more than fifty percent of the popular vote--spending most of their time trying to pay off their supporters who had gotten them elected. The "spoils system" instituted by Andrew Jackson in the 1830s was creating higher and higher levels of exploitation, and gumming up the wheels of government. With each new president, Washington, D.C. was often flooded with party sycophants and avid "office-seekers" in search of the employment they believed to be owed to them. After President James Garfield was assassinated by a disappointed "office-seeker" in 1881, his successor, Chester A. Arthur initiated reform with the passage of the Pendleton Civil Service Act and the establishment of the Civil Service Commission in 1883. This ensured that government appointments went to those people who were qualified, not purely partisan hacks.

Both the Republicans and Democrats were equally unprincipled, and the Republicans, previously keen on securing a better life for the formerly enslaved people in the south, grew tired of supporting racial equality, especially after the conclusion of Reconstruction. Republicans of the Gilded Age tended to slant instead toward policies that favored businesses, especially the railroad industry. The main point of contention between the parties at this time was the adoption of the gold standard. Starting in the latter half of the nineteenth century, many countries began to adopt the gold standard, tying the currency of that country to the value of gold. Republicans, since this would benefit big business and banking institutions, generally supported the adoption of the gold standard, while Democrats waffled at first. One of the most successful third-party movements ever in American history, the Populist Party, emerged arguing for a free silver platform instead. This would inflate prices and ease debt burdens, particularly for farmers. When the Democrats finally decided to adopt the free silver policy into their party platform, the need for the Populist Party faded, and the United States returned once more to a dual-party system. Finally, when a Republican, William McKinley, was elected president at the end of the Gilded Age, he passed the Gold Standard Act in 1900. The United States would remain on the Gold Standard until economic calamities in the twentieth century required a pivot.

THE EMPIRE OF THE UNITED STATES (1898-1945)

Towards the dawn of the twentieth century, Spain still had a colonial foothold in the North American hemisphere, particularly in Cuba. In 1895, Cubans began to resist colonial Spanish rule, and the United States, as a former colony itself, looked favorably upon the Cuban resistance. Journalists in the United States continually took the side of Cuba, highlighting the repressive and brutal measures that Spain was taking to quash the rebellion, and many Americans began to call for intervention to bring the Spanish cruelty to heel. Cuba is in close geographical proximity to the United States, and the American battleship, the *USS Maine*, was dispatched to protect American business and property interests on the island. When the *USS Maine* mysteriously exploded and sank in 1898 in Havana Harbor, the

American clamor to challenge Spain for its perceived misdeeds grew increasingly louder. In April of the same year, President William McKinley demanded Spanish withdrawal from Cuba, and in response, Spain issued war declarations. The United States followed suit, formally declaring war on Spain the following day.

Spain, though formerly a formidable colonial power, was woefully ill-equipped compared to the United States forces. The war, though waged on multiple fronts, was over within nine months, and Spain relinquished its control of Cuba and ceded control of the Caribbean island of Puerto Rico, the tiny Pacific island of Guam, and the Philippines to the United States. These new territories in addition to the controversial annexation of Hawaii in July, when a coup of American planters overthrew the last Hawaiian monarch, Queen Liliuokalani, established the United States as a colonial power. While some believed this to be a good thing, an extension of Manifest Destiny, with the United States spreading democracy around the world, others saw through the hypocrisy of the moment. In attempting to "rescue" other nations from European colonial powers, the Americans had become colonizers themselves. Additionally, the idea that the United States was a great bringer of freedom abroad rang hollow at a time when domestic policies and attitudes towards non-white Americans were anything but equitable and free.

THE PROGRESSIVE ERA

While the United States was wrestling with the concept of becoming an imperialist nation abroad, at home, the government's ineffectiveness and negligent leniency towards big business were coming to a close. As the country moved out of the Gilded Age and into the Progressive Era, many strides were made to protect workers and consumers, but it should be noted that many progressives at the time had a very narrow definition of who deserved a better and safer life. Social Darwinism continued to be in vogue, and eugenics rose in popularity until the advent of World War II. So while the reforms of the Progressive Era had a positive net effect on the country, it was a time of advancement for white, male workers. Women, Black, Asian, and Hispanic workers were left out in the cold.

The strange dichotomy of progressive policies and regressive beliefs was exemplified in the behaviors of both President Theodore Roosevelt and President Woodrow Wilson, two well-known leaders from the time. Within the country, Roosevelt's reputation for reigning in big business dubbed him as a "trust buster." His Square Deal was enacted to protect consumers, control corporations, and conserve the natural wilderness in the United States. In a sharp reversal from the permissive attitudes of the Gilded Age presidents, the government sought to protect the populace from predatory and purely profit-seeking corporations with landmark legislation like the Pure Food and Drug Act in 1906. Meanwhile, Wilson's presidency saw the creation of the Clayton Antitrust Act in 1914, as well as the formation of the Federal Reserve and the Federal Trade Commission. Both presidents seemed interested in creating a more equitable nation and lowering the impact that one wealthy business could have on the entirety of the United States. Yet the question remains, more equitable for whom?

Social Darwinism and ideas about eugenics continued to flourish and forced sterilizations occurred throughout the era. By 1907, the state of Indiana had a formal eugenics law that allowed for the sterilization of criminals and the mentally disabled. Miscegenation was explicitly outlawed throughout the country. In the south, Jim Crow policies raged on during both of their presidencies, making life hellish for Black Americans. Under President Wilson, the KKK had a horrifying resurgence, thanks in large part to the racist and inflammatory rhetoric seen in the country's first major box office hit, D.W. Griffith's *The Birth of a Nation*. Wilson himself screened the film at the White House, and there is photographic evidence from 1925 of hooded Klansmen marching on the National Mall in Washington, D.C. Nativism continued, with anti-immigrant sentiment especially toward Asians, fueling the restrictive Immigration Act of 1917 and the National Quota Law of 1921.

WORLD WAR I

Abroad, Roosevelt continued to seek naval dominance through the creation of a military base at Pearl Harbor in the new American territory of Hawaii, and through the acquisition of a strip of land in Central America that would become the Panama Canal. Later, during Wilson's first term, World War I erupted in Europe. Aside from sending supplies and money to Great Britain, Wilson largely remained isolationist, continuing a tradition that stretched back to George Washington's refusal to enmesh the young country in the French Revolution. However, once Wilson entered his second term in office, popular opinion towards American involvement in the massive European conflict began to change, thanks in large part to a successful British propaganda campaign that convinced the American public that the Germans were bloodthirsty, warmongering brutes who would happily invade the North American continent, once they were through in Europe. This imagery, coupled with the discovery of the Zimmerman Telegram--a telegram intercepted by British intelligence from the German government to the Mexican government detailing a loose plan to attack the United States through its southern border--led to the eventual end of isolationism. The United States dove into the fray of the Great War in 1917.

After the Allied Powers of the United Kingdom, France, the United States, and Italy were victorious over the Central Powers of Germany, Austria-Hungary, the Ottoman Empire, and Bulgaria, peace was hammered out in the 1919 Treaty of Versailles. Although some good came out of the treaty, the League of Nations, a precursor to the United Nations, was established, the overly punitive actions taken toward the German nation are widely thought to have set the stage for Hitler's ascendency and World War II. It seemed as though the United States had left her isolationist tendencies behind since the League of Nations was largely President Wilson's brainchild, but some exclusionary behaviors remained. The American government could never reach a quorum on whether or not to become a member nation, and thus, the United States never formally joined.

THE ROARING TWENTIES & THE GREAT DEPRESSION

As the fog of war lifted, the pendulum in the country began to swing away from the on-paper progressive policies that dominated the first two decades of the twentieth century. Whether by the mercurial nature of the American public or by the carefully crafted tug-of-war the Founding Fathers drafted into the government's DNA, American politics never seems to have the staying power to hold in one direction for too long. Republican Presidents Warren G. Harding and Calvin Coolidge were fiscal conservatives, pursuing laissez-faire economic policies similar to those of the Gilded Age, and this combined with new financial innovations led to a decade-long boom in the stock market, known colloquially as the "Roaring Twenties."

Despite the capricious tendencies of American economic and political policy, some things remain constant. Xenophobic sentiments in the nation continued and intensified throughout the Roaring Twenties. The fall of Russian Tsar Nicholas II and the subsequent Bolshevik takeover of Russia ignited intense American anxiety about communism that continues into the present day. Worry that communism would spread to the United States via immigrants, and a deep concern that America was becoming less "American" led to a continuation of anti-immigrant legislation.

All bubbles will pop, and the ballooning stock market of 1920s America was no exception. On October 24,

1929, the market nosedived into a massive crash, and the excess of the previous decade gave way to one of the darkest economic periods in the history of the United States: the Great Depression. Although the presiding president, Herbert Hoover, was unfairly painted as a heartless leader who cared little about the suffering of his populace--ramshackle communities of tents populated by those financially decimated by the Great Depression were dubbed "Hoovervilles"--his policies did attempt to reverse the fiscal calamity enveloping the nation. He initiated the construction of the Hoover Dam in Nevada and instructed Congress to investigate the causes of the Great Depression. These findings would coalesce into the Glass-Steagall Act, signed into law by his successor, which separated commercial and investment banking and created the Federal Deposit Insurance Corporation (FDIC). The Glass-Steagall Act has been an important part of protecting American consumers until large portions were repealed in 1999. Possibly, the repeal of this legislation contributed, at least in part, to the Great Recession of the early 2000s. Unfortunately for Hoover, his policies did nothing to right the economic ship of the country, and the passage of the Smoot-Hawley Tariff in 1930, meant to protect American trade interests, backfired and further harmed the economy.

Naturally, Hoover lost reelection to Franklin Delano Roosevelt, a Democrat whose controversial ideas--many of which never made it through Congress--had a large hand in creating the modern social welfare system present within the United States today. His New Deal legislation greatly expanded the power of the executive branch, and with his popular "Fireside Chats," radio speeches to the American people, he became one of the first presidents to truly utilize modern technology to reach his voters. Even though the New Deal reshaped the way Americans viewed their government, coming to see government intervention as something necessary in times of trouble, it was the economic boom accompanied by increased production for World War II, not the New Deal, that finally pulled the United States out of its downward economic spiral.

WORLD WAR II

After a humiliating defeat and devastating peace terms at the Treaty of Versailles, Germany was primed for the rise of a demagogue. Gaining the reins of the German government in the early 1930s, Adolf Hitler began a campaign of aggression that most of Europe largely ignored at first, out of fear of repeating the carnage of the Great War. Eventually, the United Kingdom and France declared war on Germany after Hitler invaded

Poland in 1939. The United States, hesitant once again to embroil itself in another bloody European conflict, sent money and aid to the Allied Powers but did not formally enter World War II until Germany's ally, Japan, bombed Pearl Harbor, Hawaii in 1941. Despite fighting for freedom and democracy abroad, the United States once again continued to engage in oppression at home. With Roosevelt's Executive Order 9066, Japanese-Americans were incarcerated in internment camps out of fear and suspicion, believing their loyalty to be compromised by their ethnicity. Although there was plenty of anti-German sentiment throughout the country, why were Americans of German descent not similarly detained?

With Roosevelt's sudden death at the start of his fourth term in April of 1945 towards the tail end of World War II, his vice president, Harry S. Truman assumed the presidency and the responsibilities of war that came along with it. Hitler's suicide a few short weeks after Roosevelt's death effectively ended the war in Europe, with V-E (Victory in Europe) Day formally declared on May 8, 1945. Several months later, Truman authorized dropping the atomic bombs on Hiroshima and Nagasaki in Japan, effectively ending the Pacific Theater of World War II with V-J (Victory over Japan) Day occurring on September 2, 1945.

The United States had managed to avoid the massive infrastructure damage suffered by Europe, and was now the sole atomic power in the world, holding unprecedented global strength. When the United Nations was established shortly after World War II to replace the League of Nations, there was no question that the United States was the superpower in charge, supplanting the European powers that had been so decimated by both World Wars I and II. The globe entered the Atomic Age with the United States at the head of the table.

6

THE POSTWAR ERA (1945-1980)

Dropping the atomic bombs on Hiroshima and Nagasaki had ended World War II at a terrible cost, and the American psyche did not emerge unscathed. Fears of nuclear retaliation and bomb drills made an apocalyptic ending seem entirely plausible and imminent. In a period of unprecedented economic boom and prosperity, the nation was tangled in webs of paranoia, panic, and conflict. The deep American fright of communism, with its seeds planted in the early 1900s and nurtured into full bloom by the aggression of the USSR in the years following World War II, became the driving force of much of the domestic and foreign policy for the second half of the twentieth century. Quality of life and life expectancy continued to grow, but racial inequalities and a cycle of progress and accompanying backlash colored daily American life.

Directly after the conclusion of World War II, tensions between the formerly allied USSR and the United States began to build; both sides believed the other to be a fundamental threat to their existence, seeing communism and capitalism as diametrically opposed. Out of this fear, the Domino Theory, the idea that if one country became communist, another would follow in suit, falling like dominos. This resulted in Truman Doctrine, a United States policy to contain and cut off communism, preventing its spread. This led to both the proxy wars in Korea from 1950 to 1953 and Vietnam from 1955 to 1975, as well as various other armed skirmishes like the disastrous Bay of Pigs Invasion in 1961, or the nerve-racking Cuban Missile Crisis in 1962.

Though George Washington had warned the American public about the danger of political parties and accompanying firebrands over one hundred years prior, a "cunning, ambitious, and unprincipled man" named Joseph McCarthy managed to capture the public eye, utilizing anxieties over communism to further his agenda. During the Second Red Scare, a senator from Wisconsin claimed to have a list of known communists who were working in the government. Utilizing the House Un-American Activities Committee which had been formed in 1938, McCarthy busied himself going after suspected communists for several years. No proof was ever found, and after McCarthy went after the United States Army, he was censured by the Senate in 1954 for grossly overstepping his bounds.

Terror continued to grip the nation when Sputnik I, a Soviet satellite, glittered across the sky in 1957, as a new frontier of potential conflict became apparent. In response, the United States formed the National Aeronautics and Space Administration (NASA) to push the "Space Race" forward, and be the first nation to put a man on the moon. This was successfully done in a little over a decade, and Neil Armstrong became the first man on the moon in 1969.

CIVIL RIGHTS

As in many moments before, the United States saw itself as a defender of freedom and democracy abroad, standing against the evils of the Soviet Union and communism, but neglecting to notice the failings at home. For years, Jim Crow policies had languished in the southern United States, depriving Black citizens of basic civil rights. Black citizens lived in fear of violence from white citizens and law enforcement. Through the 1960s and 1970s, great strides were made by civil rights activists and leaders like Martin Luther King and John

Lewis, whose tireless work ensured the passage of much-needed legislation like the Civil Rights Act of 1964 and the Voting Rights Act of 1965. This coupled with the rise of Black power leaders like Malcolm X, Stokely Carmichael, and Huey Long forced the United States into another long-overdue racial reckoning.

Many white Americans, desperately uncomfortable when faced with the Civil Rights movement, felt that they were going to lose control of what they perceived to be "their" country. The backlash was inevitable, and political parties started to fall on increasingly racialized lines. Republicans had drifted away from their abolitionist roots as early as the 1880s, beginning to favor big business. Democrats, on the other hand, thanks to the presidency of Franklin D. Roosevelt, had come to represent a larger governmental intervention in all facets of life. Many white citizens in the south had only remained Democrats because of legacy ties to the party. It was becoming clear that the parties no longer represented the factions of American society they had originally been created to serve. As Black Americans moved away from the Republican Party after Democrat presidents John F. Kennedy and Lyndon B. Johnson had presided over popular changes for Black citizens, the Republican Party began to appeal to white southerners. The result was something called the "southern strategy." Though first employed by presidential hopeful Barry

Goldwater, it was successfully implemented by Richard Nixon in 1968. Calling his voting bloc the "silent majority" and promising "law and order," Nixon railed against social change and called white southerners to the ballot box by promising them a return to order. For them, this meant no more allowance of protests, and a chance to "take back" their country. This was not the last time these sentiments became the rallying cry of an American political movement.

Though Nixon eventually left office in disgrace after the Watergate Scandal, he is known for the establishment of the Environmental Protection Agency and the prohibition of gender-based discrimination through the Education Amendments of 1972 (also known as Title IX). He was also the president responsible for extracting the United States out of the catastrophic quagmire of the Vietnam War. Here again, as with every moment of American history, there is righteousness and wickedness tangled together.

7

THE UNITED STATES IN THE MODERN ERA (1980-PRESENT DAY)

In 1980, Ronald Reagan sailed into office with a massive electoral victory over incumbent President Jimmy Carter. Carter's failure to solve the financial woes of a slumping economy coupled with an oil crisis that stung American drivers at the gas station cost him the presidency. Reagan is both deeply loved and deeply hated by different sectors of the American public. His promises to "make America great again" were born out via tax cuts and deregulation, which arguably allowed for much of the financial success of the 1980s. He effectively ended the Cold War, signing the Intermediate-Range Nuclear Forces (INF) Treaty with the USSR. Additionally, he was a brilliant orator with a gift for painting inspiring and aspiring images with his words. Much of the positive rhetoric about the United States in the current American lexicon can be traced back to him. However, he also slashed government funding for low-income housing, food stamps, and school lunch programs, vilified social welfare programs through the factually false and racist trope of "welfare queens," and largely ignored the HIV/AIDS epidemic until it was impossible to look away. His intensification of the War on Drugs initiated a surge of mass incarceration, doubling the American prison population during his two terms, and the extent of his involvement in the Iran-Contra Scandal is still quite controversial and largely unknown.

Though his economic policies, often known as Reaganomics, were popular and facilitated waves of economic growth throughout the 1980s, it tripled the debt and was somewhat unsustainable. Upon realizing the untenable nature of Reagan's policies, his successor and former vice president, George Bush was forced to renege on his campaign promises of "no new taxes," which greatly harmed his national popularity, and potentially cost him his reelection bid.

With the Cold War moving into America's rearview window, and the USSR's collapse, a power vacuum opened up in the Middle East, which had previously been under a degree of Soviet influence. In the early 1990s, Saddam Hussein, the dictator of Iraq, invaded

Kuwait in a bid to gain access to the oil resources in the region. The United States, alongside the United Nations Security Council, urged Hussein to pull back, since the United States had a friendly diplomatic relationship with Kuwait, as well as a vested interest in the distribution of oil resources in the Middle East. When Hussein refused, the United States moved on Iraq with a thirty-five nation coalition, marking the onset of the First Gulf War. Ultimately, it was a military victory for the United States, but the nation's continually increasing demand for oil would further enmesh the fates of the United States and the Middle East moving into the twenty-first century.

Although the United States had fought alongside allies before, the massive coalition pulled together for Gulf War I was illustrative of the increasing globalization of the time. The advent of the internet further connected the political and economic fates of all the nations of the world, which while wonderful for lowering barriers for trade--as was done with the North American Free Trade Agreement (NAFTA) under President Bill Clinton--it also meant that financial crises would be felt worldwide. In this newly interconnected reality, a new breed of enemy burst forth: global terrorism. The United States felt the weight of this with the September 11 attacks in 2001.

After a period of brief patriotic reunification in wake of the terror attacks, the United States swung back into its pattern of progress and backlash. The questions of security versus freedom, who pays the tax burden, and just what should be done about healthcare have raged on for the better part of twenty years. The political parties are hotly divided, with many members of the party in the legislative branch opposing the sitting president vowing to do whatever it takes to block his agenda. The executive branch continues to change party hands frequently and making the country's role on the global stage questionable. Even the nation's staunchest allies cannot rely on one administration to fulfill the promises of their predecessor. On the issue of climate change alone, the United States has shifted its bearing unceasingly. From Clinton to Biden, the country has joined worldwide efforts to combat climate change three times and pulled out twice in the last thirty or so years.

The Founding Fathers' prescient concerns about political parties were well-founded. The polarization of the nation has reached such a stage of toxicity that many Americans wonder if this could be the end of the Republic. The United States remains a global superpower, but the rise of economic and military challengers like China will likely test the mettle of the nation in the coming years. However, if history has illustrated anything, it is that the United States has and always will be a land of wealth and poverty, opportunity and devastation, freedom and subjugation, advancement and retreat. All that citizens can hope is that it keeps stumbling forward, unceasingly maneuvering through the contradictions, trying to fulfill the great promise that "all men are created equal."

LEAVE A QUICK REVIEW!

I hope you enjoyed this book. If you did, I'd appreciate it if you left a review on Amazon. Your reviews are the lifeblood of my business and I incorporate the feedback into future books.

To leave a review, go to:
Amazon.com/review/create-review?
&asin=B094HCS545

Or scan with your camera:

OTHER BOOKS BY DOMINIC HAYNES

(AVAILABLE ON AMAZON & AUDIBLE)

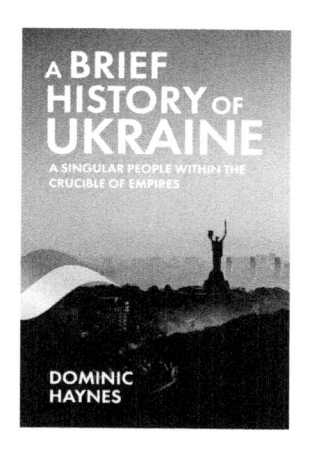

A Brief History of Ukraine: A Singular People Within the Crucible of Empires

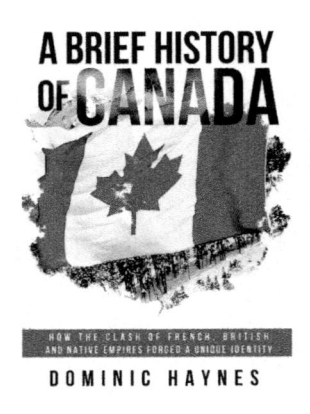

A Brief History of Canada: How the Clash of French, British and Native Empires Forged a Unique Identity

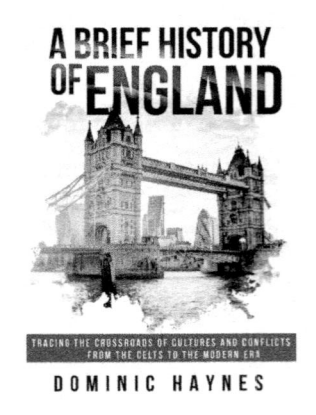

A Brief History of England: Tracing the Crossroads of Cultures and Conflicts from the Celts to the Modern Era

REFERENCES

"Have You No Sense of Decency?" (n.d.) *Powers & Procedures, Investigations.* The United States Senate. https://www.senate.gov/about/powers-procedures/investigations/mccarthy-hearings/have-you-no-sense-of-decency.htm

"KKK Parade" (1925, August 8). *KKK Parade.* Library of Congress. https://www.loc.gov/pictures/item/2016851326/

Boissoneault, L. (2017, January 26). *How the 19th-Century Know-Nothing Party Reshaped American Politics.* The Smithsonian Magazine. https://www.smithsonianmag.com/history/immigrants-conspiracies-and-secret-society-launched-american-nativism-180961915/

Editors, T. (2019, June 6). *Louisiana Purchase.* History. https://www.history.com/topics/westward-expansion/louisiana-purchase

Editors, T. (2019, May 16). *Joseph McCarthy.* History. https://www.history.com/topics/cold-war/joseph-mccarthy

Editors, T. (2019, November 4). *Missouri Compromise.* History. https://www.history.com/topics/abolitionist-movement/missouri-compromise

Editors, T. (2020, April 23). *War of 1812.* History. https://www.history.com/topics/war-of-1812/war-of-1812

Editors, T. (2020, February 21). *Spanish-American War.* History. https://www.history.com/topics/early-20th-century-us/spanish-american-war

Editors, T. (2020, January 14). *Americans Overthrow Hawaiian Monarchy.* History. https://www.history.com/this-day-in-history/americans-overthrow-hawaiian-monarchy

Editors, T. (2020, January 17). *Persian Gulf War.* History. https://www.history.com/topics/middle-east/persian-gulf-war

Editors, T. (2020, July 30). *Delegates Sign the Declaration of Independence.* History. https://www.history.com/this-day-in-history/delegates-sign-declaration-of-independence

REFERENCES

Editors, T. (2020, March 3). *Treaty of Versailles*. History. https://www.history.com/topics/world-war-i/treaty-of-versailles-1

Editors, T. (n.d.). *1907 Indiana Eugenics Law*. Indiana Historical Bureau. https://www.in.gov/history/state-historical-markers/find-a-marker/1907-indiana-eugenics-law/

Editors, T. (n.d.). *The Adams Presidency*. U.S. History Online Textbook. https://www.ushistory.org/us/19d.asp

Editors, T. (n.d.). *The American Experience: Andrew Carnegie: The Richest Man in the World, The Strike at Homestead Mill*. Public Broadcasting Service. https://www.pbs.org/wgbh/americanexperience/features/carnegie-strike-homestead-mill/

Freidel, F. and H. Sidey (2006). *Herbert Hoover*. The White House. https://www.whitehouse.gov/about-the-white-house/presidents/herbert-hoover/

Keegan, J. (2000). *The First World War*. Penguin Random House.

Lioudis, N. (2021, April 27). *What is the Gold Standard?*. Investopedia. https://www.investopedia.com/ask/answers/09/gold-standard.asp

Maues, J. (2013, November 22). *Banking Act of 1933 (Glass-Steagall)*. Federal Reserve History. https://www.federalreservehistory.org/essays/glass-steagall-act

Washington, G. (1792, August 26). *Creating the United States*. Library of Congress. https://www.loc.gov/exhibits/creating-the-united-states/ext/transcription74.html

Printed in Great Britain
by Amazon